W9-BNO-183

Aretha

THE QUEEN *of* SOUL

Aretha

THE QUEEN *of* SOUL

A Life in Photographs

Introduction & Text by **MEREDITH OCHS**

Photo Editor **CHRISTOPHER MEASOM**

STERLING
New York

STERLING
New York

An Imprint of Sterling Publishing Co., Inc.
1166 Avenue of the Americas
New York, NY 10036

STERLING and the distinctive Sterling logo are registered
trademarks of Sterling Publishing Co., Inc.

Text © 2018 Meredith Ochs
Cover © 2018 Sterling Publishing, Co; Inc.

ISBN: 978-1-4549-3458-5

Distributed in Canada by Sterling Publishing Co., Inc.
c/o Canadian Manda Group, 664 Annette Street
Toronto, Ontario M6S 2C8, Canada
Distributed in the United Kingdom by GMC Distribution Services
Castle Place, 166 High Street, Lewes, East Sussex BN7 1XU, England
Distributed in Australia by NewSouth Books
45 Beach Street, Coogee, NSW 2034, Australia

For information about custom editions, special sales, and premium and
corporate purchases, please contact Sterling Special Sales at 800-805-5489
or specialsales@sterlingpublishing.com.

Manufactured in Canada

2 4 6 8 10 9 7 5 3 1

sterlingpublishing.com

Interior design by Timothy Shaner, NightandDayDesign.biz
Cover design by Elizabeth Mihaltse Lindy

Cover photographs by CSU Archives/Everett Collection/Alamy (front);
Pat Benic-POOL/CNP/ZUMA Wire/Alamy Live News (back)

Picture Credits — see page 138

CONTENTS

· · · · · · · · · · ·

INTRODUCTION

"A FORCE THAT CAN
LIGHT A ROOM"

As an artist, Aretha Franklin is loved and revered, though many fans don't grasp the full scope of her musical genius. Her voice is evident, an octave-leaping mezzo soprano capable of dizzying, melismatic runs. Mostly self-taught, Aretha played by ear with the kind of perfect pitch that allowed her to re-create anything she heard, note for note, before she reached grade school. She didn't really read music and didn't need it to record songs; the breadth of her musical knowledge was astonishing. So brilliant were her piano skills that pianists like Elton John proclaimed her to be a favorite. She was a master of phrasing and improvisation, toying with rhythm, vamping with spontaneous lyrics and scatting, taking songs where no one else could, her vocal pyrotechnics never obscuring her soulful delivery. Everything she sang—and she pretty much sang everything, including gospel, blues, R&B, jazz, pop, hip-hop, opera, country, folk—resonated with that elusive quality. "It's like electricity—we don't really know what it is. But it's a force that can light a room," Ray Charles said, attempting to define the word *soul*. There's a reason she was called the Queen of Soul and will never be dethroned.

For music royalty, however, Aretha was distinctly "down-home," as Smokey Robinson and many others who knew her observed. She rarely gave interviews, and sometimes didn't appear at all. When she did, she was often covered in sequins, jewels, and furs, yet she was "of the people." She loved to cook and did so for friends, family, collaborators, and writers visiting her at home; on television shows like *Live with Kelly and Michael* and *Oprah*; and with the domestic diva herself, Martha Stewart. Though a reserved conversationalist, she spoke in vernacular that made it clear she had an ear to the street. The album title *Who's Zoomin' Who?* was something she casually

Page ii: Aretha Franklin at the Chicago Theater in Chicago, Illinois, January 1986. **Page iv:** Aretha Franklin. **Opposite:** Aretha Franklin, c. 1965.

said while talking on the phone with producer Narada Michael Walden about checking out guys (and vice versa) in a nightclub. She was hip. She had a sense of what the public wanted to hear that enabled her nearly six decades of artistic reinvention and influence.

And she was funny, a trait she rarely exhibited but that was evident at sporadic moments, when she'd joke with her band onstage, or during informal chats, or in her film and television cameos. "The Queen had a wry, skeptical eye on the world, but once you got her laughing you were in," Dan Aykroyd, her costar in the *Blues Brothers* movies, said. A skilled impressionist, she reserved her best for close friends and family offstage but occasionally included a "diva medley" in her act, nailing the vocal styles and facial expressions of her contemporaries like Mavis Staples and Gladys Knight, even donning an electric pink marabou coat to mimic the frequently feathered Diana Ross.

Aretha was also habitually and quietly generous. From her 1960s tour with Harry Belafonte to help fund Martin Luther King Jr. and the Southern Christian Leadership Conference, to the numerous benefit concerts she played and donations she made throughout the decades, to offering hotel rooms and food to Flint families during their water crisis, she retained the notion of charity from her religious upbringing.

The church shaped her life early on, and it remained a fundamental part of who she was. Her family followed the preaching career of its patriarch, Reverend C. L. Franklin, moving from Memphis, Tennessee, where Aretha was born in 1942, to Buffalo, New York, and then to Detroit, Michigan. Her father's philandering led her mother, Barbara Siggers (herself a gifted singer), back to Buffalo when Aretha was six, leaving C. L. Franklin a single dad. Siggers's 1952 death had a devastating effect on the four kids, especially Aretha. "After her mama died, the whole family wanted for love," Mahalia Jackson said.

Music, however, was Aretha's salvation and doctrine, and it put her on the road from the time she was twelve, singing in churches and arenas around the country to warm up the crowd for her famous father's impassioned sermons. Throughout the 1950s, she experienced the impact of segregation and Jim Crow—the restaurants and hotels that wouldn't accept black patrons or allow them restroom access, and the information network by which they found places where they'd be welcomed, such as Gulf service stations ("We didn't buy gas where we could not use the restrooms," she explained). She perceived the power of her father's magnetism, along with the freewheeling lifestyle of touring musicians, its paradoxical relationship to religion, and how to inhabit both worlds. In every way, there was only one outcome for Aretha—gifted with preternatural talent, scarred by loss, deeply moved by a sense of social justice, growing up around her country's most active civil rights leaders and some of its greatest musicians—she was going to be a legend.

Opposite: Aretha Franklin in a promotional still, c. 1967.

PART ONE

Detroit

DETROIT'S NUMBER
ONE DAUGHTER

Before the world knew her by her first name, she was Ree Ree, peering from the second-floor bedroom window of her family's Detroit home to catch a glimpse of whoever was walking up the path to visit her father, Reverend C. L. Franklin. While he entertained, she'd sit at the top of the staircase, sometimes with sisters Erma and Carolyn or brother Cecil, listening to the adults converse and music being played. If it was very late and she'd already fallen asleep, her dad might wake her and bring her downstairs to sing for company.

"Company" often meant luminaries. Civil rights leader Martin Luther King Jr., jazz-piano great Art Tatum, gospel icon Mahalia Jackson, Soul Stirrer-turned-secular singer Sam Cooke, and countless more were friends and cohorts of the Reverend, whose fame had transcended the ecumenical world. Charismatic and progressive, Franklin was already making a name for himself when he was brought to Detroit to lead the New Bethel Baptist Church in 1946. His sermons were enthralling, providing African American congregants much-needed inspiration during the Great Migration and the long struggle for equality. During his years as a preacher in Memphis and Buffalo, he'd used radio as a medium, reaching out to a broader audience via his own show. In his newly adopted city, he became a recording artist.

When local indie record pioneer Joe Von Battle began pressing Franklin's sermons on vinyl for his J.V.B. label, the Reverend's star rose further. Von Battle's record store and studio were on Hastings Street in the part of town known as Black Bottom (named for its fertile topsoil when it was mostly farms), a flourishing African American business and entertainment district. He recorded numerous locals, including John Lee Hooker, after the influential bluesman had relocated to Detroit

> "She was first Detroit's, then America's, then the world's."
>
> —DR. E. L. BRANCH, THIRD NEW HOPE CHURCH

Previous page: During a recording session at the Atlantic Records studio in New York, January 1969. **Opposite:** A portrait, c. 1964.

to work at the Ford Motor Company (Hooker is standing in front of the Hastings Street store on the cover of his 1993 album *The Legendary Modern Recordings 1948–1954*). The Reverend's albums sold well, sometimes outpacing the blues artists, and demand grew to other cities. Within the decade, Von Battle would be recording Aretha as well.

The Franklin family first landed in Detroit's North End on Boston Boulevard, a stately stretch of road with a grassy, tree-lined median, at the corner of Oakland. Compared to most of the area, it was a mansion. The Reverend couldn't have chosen a better neighborhood in which to settle with his musically inclined kids; a six-year-old Smokey Robinson lived around the corner on Belmont Street, down the road from him was Diana Ross, and a block or two beyond were the Four Tops, all of them young and eager to perform.

Even among these future Motown stars, though, Aretha stood out. Robinson, "a sandbox friend" who became a lifelong friend, as she later mused, was amazed by the grandeur of the Franklin home and its contents, the likes of which he hadn't seen—"oil paintings, velvet tapestries, silk curtains, mahogany cabinets filled with ornate objects of silver and gold . . . an elaborate Emerson TV," he'd recount of his first visit. But he was more stunned by the family wunderkind. "We go into the house and we're walking around, and I hear a piano being played and somebody singing," he says. "I open this door and here's little Aretha Franklin . . . playing piano and singing damn near like she sings now."

That voice. Even a nonbeliever could hear something divine in a voice that came out of her almost fully realized, but it was her father's

church where she started singing, and where she made her first recordings for J.V.B. Aretha was fourteen when she recorded the nine tracks that would later be released as *Songs of Faith*, but her voice is uncannily mature. By then, she'd already lived an adult life, having lost her mother, giving birth to two sons (she'd have two more in her twenties), dropping out of Northern High, and traveling the country as an opening act for her dad.

Touring had a profound impact on Aretha, but she was still shaped by Detroit. She

Above: Aretha Franklin with her first husband and manager, Ted White, c. 1961. **Opposite**: A "preaching and singing" concert poster from 1960 features the Reverend C. L. Franklin and his daughter Aretha. **Following pages:** Aretha Franklin with Ted White in Rome, 1968.

SOMETHING DIFFERENT ● PREACHING AND SINGING

REV. C. L. FRANKLIN
AND HIS DAUGHTER
ARETHA FRANKLIN
OF DETROIT

Rev. C. L. FRANKLIN

STAPLE
SINGERS
OF CHICAGO

STAPLE SINGERS

Miss SAMMIE BRYANT

MISS BRYANT THE LITTLE LADY WITH THE BIG VOICE (3 FEET TALL) OF DETROIT

HOWARD HI-SCHOOL
CHATTANOOGA ● 8:00 P. M.
MON. APR. 4

ADMISSION: $1.00 ADVANCE ● $1.25 AT DOOR
H. NASH PRESENTATION SOUTHERN POSTER PRINTING CO., ATLANTA, GA.

attended its public schools, skated in its historic roller rinks, and was influenced by its music scene. When the Franklins moved from North End to an even more spectacular, nearly six-thousand-square-foot home on LaSalle Street in walking distance of Motown's Studio A, Aretha would stop by the small white house emblazoned with the HITSVILLE U.S.A. sign, crossing what is now Rosa Parks Boulevard (Parks moved to the area after fleeing the south in the late 1950s). "I would just go over to the studio to see who was recording, just

to say hello, maybe to Smokey or Mary Wells, or someone who I was friends with," she said. The up-and-coming Motown Records wanted Aretha, but she signed with New York–based Columbia, the prestige label that was home to Bessie Smith, Billie Holiday, and family friends Mahalia Jackson and Dinah Washington (she'd later record an album of Washington's songs for Columbia after the singer's death at thirty-nine).

Though she never recorded for Motown, Aretha remains Detroit's number one daughter, because she never really left. Even during stretches in New York and Los Angeles, she often traveled home. She bought and held on to properties in and around the city for decades—including the Colonial she shared with her first husband, Ted White, on Sorrento Avenue between Seven and Eight Mile Roads, and the family home on LaSalle, which she finally sold in 2013 (at the time of her death, she still owned at least five properties in the region). As a Columbia recording artist, she returned home for a ten-night stint at the Flame Show Bar in the city's Paradise Valley neighborhood beginning on May 3, 1963. It was billed as her hometown nightclub debut, on the same stage that hosted Holiday, Washington, T-Bone Walker, Moms Mabley, Louis Jordan, LaVern Baker, and many more.

Detroit showed even more respect for Aretha after her late 1960s commercial breakthrough. At Cobo Hall, in front of an ecstatic hometown crowd of twelve thousand, including her father and Martin Luther King Jr., Detroit mayor Jerome Cavanaugh declared February 16, 1968, to be "Aretha Franklin Day." Five years earlier, King had test-driven his "I Have a Dream" speech at Cobo a few

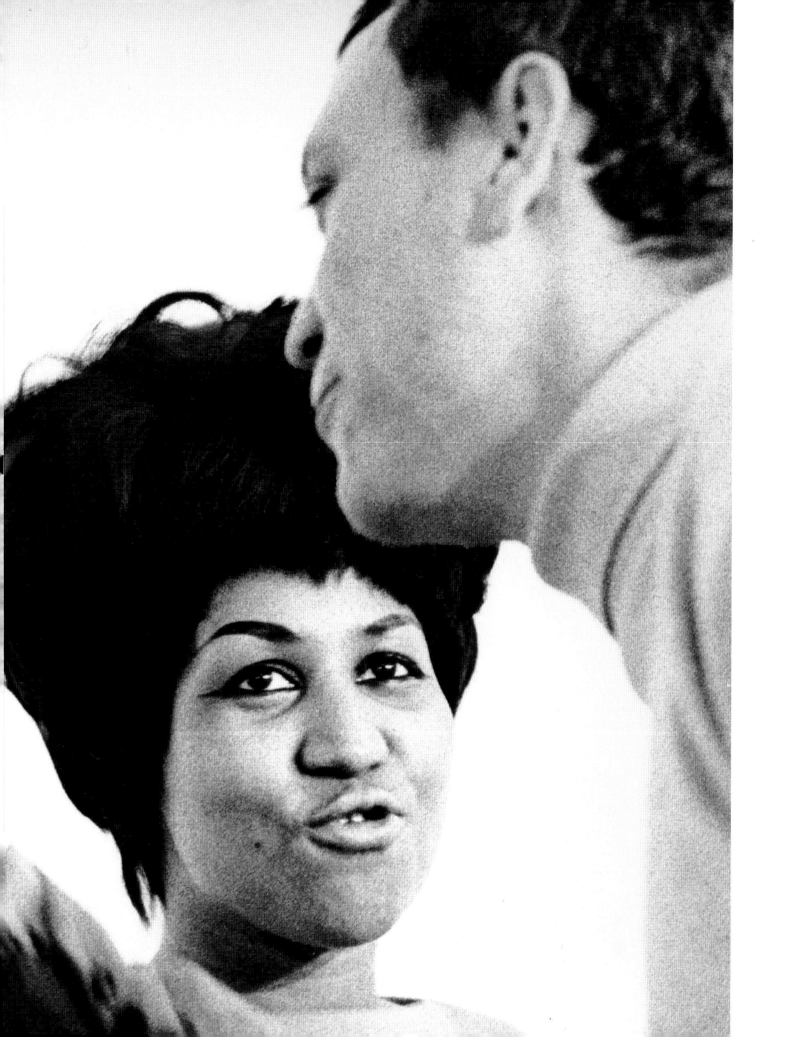

weeks before he delivered the historic version in Washington, DC. He and Reverend Franklin had just led 125,000 people down Woodward Avenue in the Detroit Walk to Freedom, the city's largest civil rights demonstration.

In 1968, though, the city was still reeling from the previous summer's 12th Street Riot, one of the worst in American history. Michigan governor George Romney called in the state's Army National Guard; President Lyndon Johnson called in two Army Airborne divisions. Up until then, Mayor Cavanaugh had been considered a Democratic presi-

> "[Our father] would drag her out of bed and she'd go down there and play for the stars. And they considered her a star once they heard her."
>
> —ERMA FRANKLIN

dential hopeful, but his political loss paled in comparison to the death and destruction left in the riot's wake. Even Joe Von Battle's record shop, which he'd moved to 12th Street after his original location was gutted to make room for the Chrysler Freeway, was destroyed, along with priceless unreleased recordings. It never reopened, and he died five years later. So many of Detroit's thriving black neighborhoods, including North End, Paradise Valley, and Black Bottom, were essentially paved over by the building of the interstate system and so-called urban renewal projects. Riots ended

much of what was left. Aretha's music in that era spoke to a nation grappling with social change, but for Detroit, their hometown artist was as important as her message.

Aretha moved back for good in 1982. Her father, shot during a 1979 home invasion on LaSalle, was left in a persistent coma, and she was in a period of personal and professional transition. She divorced her second husband, actor Glynn Turman, in 1984, the same year Reverend Franklin died. Conversely, her career took off again in the 1980s. She also developed an acute fear of flying during this time; a shaky trip in a prop plane from Atlanta to Detroit left her ground-bound for the rest of her life, traveling with her entourage in a luxury bus. She bought an expansive manse in Bloomfield Hills, a tony Detroit suburb, installed heavy bars on the windows, and at times lived like a recluse.

Yet she had a way of showing up locally when needed and rarely missed a chance to give her city its "propers." She shot the music video for her 1985 Grammy-winning hit "Freeway of Love" in front of Doug's Body Shop, a car-themed bar on Woodward Avenue between Eight and Nine Mile. The video celebrated the city and the auto industry, with glimpses of Big Three signage, dancers dressed as auto workers, and a quick shot of the old Motown studio house, ending with Aretha driving into the sunset in white furs and a pink Cadillac. In 1987, WrestleMania III came to Pontiac, Michigan, around five miles from her house, and there was Aretha on a grand piano with three backup singers, opening the show with "America the Beautiful" for a live audience

Opposite: In concert, c. 1985.

of more than 93,000 (the WWE also used "Who's Zoomin' Who?" as a theme song). When WrestleMania returned to Michigan two decades later, she reprised her act.

From the dawn of her fame, Aretha gave concerts to raise money for causes she cared about, and throughout her life she contributed to Detroit's food banks and churches, especially New Bethel, where she appeared at periodic revivals that included catfish, ribs, and greens for all. "Aretha gave to three or four churches $10,000–$12,000 at a time," Rev. Robert Smith Jr., New Bethel's pastor, said. "She was all about feeding the poor, and on top of that she would have programs where you could come in and eat from four in the evening to one o'clock in the morning." She also supported local businesses that she liked. A customer of Harmony House, Michigan's largest chain of family-owned record stores, she said yes when they asked her to do a television commercial for their fiftieth anniversary in 1997; she requested that her fee be donated to a Detroit women's shelter. Her only other requirements were a limo and barbecue, which she must've enjoyed, because she went off script with an ad-libbed finger snap and sang "R-E-S-P-E-C-T" at the end of the commercial.

Aretha rooted for Detroit's home teams, too, opening events like the Tigers' game 3 of Major League Baseball's ALC championship in 2001, and the Pistons' game 5 of the NBA finals in 2004. When Super Bowl XL was held at Ford Field, she sang with Dr. John and Aaron Neville and spoke out about the fact that halftime contained no Motown talent. But the apogee of her sporting performances was the Thanksgiving game kickoff on November 24, 2016.

Seated at a grand piano, she performed the national anthem in a pompom-topped Detroit Lions ski cap with matching blue nail polish, wrapped in a chinchilla coat, with enough piano and vocal flourish to fill up four minutes and thirty-five seconds, more than twice the song's average length. The Twitterverse lit up, and the looks on the faces of the players, a mix of reverence and bafflement as it just kept going, was priceless. So was the rainbow that appeared suddenly and stretched across Ford Field during a moment of silence in her memory before the Tigers' winning game on August 21, 2018.

When she showed up for her country, Aretha often brought with her a piece of home. She performed at inaugural events for Presidents Carter, Clinton, and Obama, most memorably the 2009 inauguration of the latter, when she sang "My Country, 'Tis of Thee" beneath the infamous gray, crystal-studded bow hat designed by Motor City milliner Luke

. . . .

> "She was amongst her people, she loved her people. She stayed right here in Detroit giving us a good name. For anything that bad people could say about Detroit, we say 'Aretha Franklin' and they couldn't say a thing."
>
> —REV. ROBERT SMITH JR., NEW BETHEL BAPTIST CHURCH

. . . .

Song. Even when she wore other designers, she had longtime hairstylist Carlton Northern, a Detroit lifer, along to provide a suitable coif for her over-the-top fashions, including her now-classic performance at the 2015 Kennedy Center Honors.

When Aretha began to have serious health issues in 2010—diagnosed with pancreatic cancer, she had surgery to remove a tumor and dropped eighty-five pounds—she kept her status on lockdown but turned to Detroit's religious community, asking friend and city councilor JoAnn Watson to host a prayer vigil for her at City Hall. Aretha chose which ministers she wanted there and specified that they should be instructed "only to pray and not to talk to the press," according to Watson. Aretha never talked about being sick, as if admitting it was antithetical to fighting it. But at a 2012 benefit for Hackensack University Medical Center in New Jersey, where she sang a tremendous ninety-minute set on the banks of the Hudson River for nearly four thousand survivors and caregivers, she issued a rare statement on the subject: "Cancer patients too often feel socially isolated as a result of their disease, so building a strong sense of community and [a] support network is especially important. No one should have to go through cancer feeling alone."

Illness slowed her down, but music propped her up. Booked to perform at the thirtieth anniversary celebration of Detroit's Chene Park on August 22, 2015, she didn't make it onstage until 10:30 p.m. Her performance that night though was two hours strong, including a sprawling jazz ensemble, a wardrobe change, and a ten-minute-long version of "Bridge over Troubled Water." Situated

Opposite: Aretha Franklin, an Atlantic Records star, May 1968.

> . . . .
>
> "Aretha was complicated,
> loving, and giving. . . . Her
> faith in Detroit and its people
> is what I will remember as
> much as her voice."
>
> —DEBBIE DINGELL, US REPRESENTATIVE
> FOR MICHIGAN'S 12TH DISTRICT
>
> . . . .

by the Detroit River, where she lived the last few months of her life, Chene Park had grown to be a major entertainment hub and attraction; days after her funeral, the City Council declared its name would be changed permanently to Aretha Louise Franklin Park.

Her final full concert was the inaugural Detroit Music Weekend on June 10, 2017. Created to help bolster the local economy and celebrate Motor City music and culture, they badly needed a headliner, and Franklin wanted to help. She talked about it possibly being her last concert but didn't discuss her diminishing health, so when she kept canceling and then recommitting—including on the day of the show—it further stoked the cancer rumors. Two days before the festival, a noticeably thinner Franklin was moved to tears as she watched the naming of Aretha Franklin Way, the stretch of Madison Avenue between Witherell and Brush Streets that runs by the Detroit Opera House (see photograph on page 105). A year earlier, the section of Linwood Street near New Bethel was renamed for her father (as was nearby LaSalle Park).

The weekend of the concert was so hot that promoters worried she wouldn't make it, but at the last minute she got out of her car and took the stage. She was wearing the same gown she'd worn when she performed at Radio City Music Hall in New York to open the Tribeca Film Festival—she didn't feel well then either but showed up to launch the film about Clive Davis, the famous record executive who'd signed her to Arista in 1980 and remained a friend ever since. It had only been a couple of months since she'd appeared in the white sleeveless dress with its fluid skirt and gold beaded flowers, but it looked almost too big for her now. Still, she was radiant in her home base, her hair worn stick-straight and in a gold ombré, her large white leather handbag onstage behind her (as her handbag always was). Detroit mayor Mike Duggan awarded her a key to the city. The nearly two-hour performance, backed by a big band and full of career-spanning deep cuts, was a triumph for the diva and her city.

"The celebrated and the uncelebrated danced to the queen's music, cleaned house to the queen's music, laughed, cried, made cornbread and greens to her music, break up, make up, dream dreams to her music.

—CRISETTE ELLIS, FIRST LADY, GREATER GRACE TEMPLE

Opposite: Aretha Franklin, c. 1967. **Following pages**: With a copy of her album *Aretha Franklin: Soul '69* at the Atlantic Records studios in New York, January 1969.

66My sister was always engaged in acts of kindness and charity that went unreported. She and I would be watching the late news. There'd be a story about a woman who lost her home in a fire and the next thing you knew, Aretha was on the phone to the news station getting the woman's number. The next day she'd send her a check for thirty thousand dollars.99 —ERMA FRANKLIN

Opposite: A family portrait: Aretha Franklin (center), her father, Baptist preacher C. L. (Clarence LaVaughn), and her sister and fellow singer Carolyn, 1971.

Above: Aretha Franklin (in fur coat and hat) at the Hollywood Christmas parade with her son Kecalf Cunningham (center), her second husband, actor Glynn Turman (right), and his two children Glynn Jr. and Stephanie (left), 1978.

> **I didn't cross the line. Gospel goes with me wherever I go. Gospel is a constant with me. I just broadened my musical horizons.**
>
> —ARETHA ON HER TRANSITION FROM SACRED TO SECULAR MUSIC

Opposite: Aretha poses during the cover shoot for her 1987 gospel album *One Lord, One Faith, One Baptism*.

Following pages: Showing her love for Smokey Robinson during a rehearsal for the *Aretha Franklin: Duets* concert (benefiting the Gay Men's Health Crisis) at the Nederlander Theatre in New York, April 1993.

❝She was dynamically in tune with what was going on around her in that studio . . . it was never an ego thing at all with her. It was a music thing. She was brilliant in that way I think.❞—SPOONER OLDHAM

Opposite: A promotional photo of singer, pianist, and Queen of Soul in the early 1960s. **Above**: With producers Tom Dowd (left) and Jerry Wexler in the Atlantic Records studio during "The Weight" recording session, January 1969.

Opposite: The Queen of Soul, c. 1967. **Above:** Aretha Franklin and Ken
Cunningham at the beach, c. 1980.

Opposite: Aretha Franklin arrives in Stockholm, 1968. **Following pages:** With the Godfather of Soul, James Brown, taping *Cinemax Sessions: A Soul Session: James Brown & Friends* at the Taboo nightclub in Detroit, January 1987.

66Aretha Franklin was my dear, dear friend, my homegirl, and I loved her a lot. From seeing her as a baby singing and playing at the piano at her father's home, to her giving a rousing performance at the White House, she has always been amazing.99—BERRY GORDY

Above: Berry Gordy hugs Aretha at the Motown 50 Golden Gala Live It Again! benefit for the Motown Museum in Detroit, November 21, 2009.
Opposite: Detroit's Fox Theatre, June 22, 2012.

PART TWO

Reinvention

"SHE COULD CREATE A PICTURE
ANY WAY SHE WANTED"

Aretha's prodigious talent couldn't be contained by a single genre. She listened to all kinds of music and had a great curiosity about what was current at any given time, and her interests helped shape her artistic direction. Still, it's one thing to admire Luciano Pavarotti, but quite another to fill in for him, as she did at the 1998 Grammy Awards. "She had a gospel component to her work, but there was another side, an emotional side that she controlled through her singing," songwriter Dave Porter said. "She could take a word—a single word—and imbue it with so many degrees of meaning and shading, that it would connect with the listener and impact them directly. She was tremendously gifted in her word imagery talents. She could create a picture any way she wanted."

Aretha was inspired when her friend Sam Cooke crossed over from gospel to pop stardom as his song "You Send Me" topped the *Billboard* Hot 100 and the R&B charts in 1957 (she'd record it in 1968, four years after Cooke's death at age thirty-three). She knew Sam from her touring days on the church circuit and his visits to the Franklins' Detroit home and had a

> "There's a master class in every song that she's recorded."
>
> —JON BATISTE

lifelong crush on him—the mere mention of his name made her blush, even into her seventies. Cooke tried to convince Reverend Franklin to let Aretha sign with his label, RCA, but they held out for Columbia Records. Once Columbia's eminent talent scout/producer John Hammond heard her demo, it was a done deal; he considered her the greatest voice he'd heard since he discovered a seventeen-year-old Billie Holiday nearly three decades earlier.

Columbia saw her potential as a crossover artist when they signed her in 1960, pairing her with a number of band leaders, arrangers, and top session musicians to record standards, vocal

Previous page: Aretha Franklin backstage, c. 1980.
Opposite: Backstage before a performance at Symphony Hall in Newark, New Jersey, 1969.

jazz, show tunes, R&B, and blues. Her secular debut was *Aretha: With the Ray Bryant Combo*, and she reached the Top 40 for the first time with "Rock-a-Bye Your Baby with a Dixie Melody." In the late 1960s, she covered Tin Pan Alley songwriters such as Irving Berlin ("How Deep Is the Ocean"), George Gershwin and Irving Caesar ("Swanee"), Oscar Hammerstein and Jerome Kern ("Ol' Man River"), and Hoagy Carmichael and Johnny Mercer ("Skylark," which she revisited periodically over the decades that followed). The songbook may seem oddly unhip in hindsight, but at the time it was a conventional approach to breaking in an artist. It was also a great experience for Aretha. Though she'd grown up hearing more than just gospel, her Columbia years made her even more versatile, added structure to her improv, helped expand her phrasing, and immersed her in a professional studio setting.

After six years with the label yielded minimal success, she departed for Atlantic

. . . .

"I remember running into Sarah Vaughan, who always intimidated me. Sarah said, 'Have you heard of this Aretha Franklin girl?' I said, 'You heard her do "Skylark," didn't you?' Sarah said, 'Yes, I did, and I'm never singing that song again.'"

—ETTA JAMES

. . . .

Records, courted by label partner and producer Jerry Wexler, who thought getting her closer to rhythm and blues (a term he has been credited with creating) and a more improvisational approach to recording would better suit her. It worked, yielding more than a dozen albums in a dozen years and ten Grammys, launched by a string of impactful and timely singles. The first pair of songs from her label debut, *I Never Loved a Man the Way I Love You*, underscore the opposing sides of her romantic travails. The pleading and acquiescing to a mean, mistreating lover on the title track was followed by the proclamation of self-worth and ardent demand for "Respect," which elevated Aretha to the Queen of Soul and netted her the first two of eighteen Grammys. She'd turned Otis Redding's original into an anthem, with ad-libbed lyrics, catchy syncopation, and her backup singer sisters' unconsecrated tabernacle whooping, all supporting the indelible power of her delivery. Played in the context of late 1960s cultural and political upheaval—the fight for civil rights, women's rights, and black power along with the antiwar movement—even Aretha's relationship songs were imbued with social conscience, and her fame exploded.

The album's recording sessions exploded, too, on the very first day. Wexler set up time at FAME Studios in Muscle Shoals, Alabama, with renowned session players known as the Swampers. When trumpeter Ken Laxton, who'd been brought in from Memphis, mouthed off to Aretha's then-husband Ted White, it ended in pejorative name calling and a scuffle between White and studio owner Rick Hall, followed by White and Aretha's immediate departure (they'd later

Opposite: A publicity portrait, c. 1964.

reconvene the sessions in New York). But in that one day, they recorded "I Never Loved a Man," a sultry, seductive groove in 6/8 time. Aretha's arrangement unfolds as the song builds up from Spooner Oldham's boggy Wurlitzer keyboard, to her joining in on piano on the second verse, to the horn section (at her direction), to stinging bursts of guitar. Aretha's piano playing guided both her vocal phrasing and the band, giving the recordings a more extemporaneous sound that had a gospel-blues feel and the pull of soul music that resonated with fans.

By 1968, she was unstoppable, releasing two albums. *Aretha: Lady Soul* had yet another one-two punch with a pair of gospel-infused, career-making hits about relationships that served as double entendres for social issues: Don Covay's chooglin' "Chain of Fools," and its good-lovin' opposite "(You Make Me Feel Like) A Natural Woman," which Carole King and Gerry Goffin wrote for her, all of it embellished with guitar cameos by stylish string benders Eric Clapton, Joe South, and Bobby Womack (who'd also backed Sam Cooke). The other was *Aretha Now*, which opened with her own composition, the explosive "Think," with its dramatic key modulation and escalating "freedom" lyric.

What should've been her most triumphant year, though, was fraught. Two months after he'd been in Detroit at Cobo Hall for the proclamation of Aretha Franklin Day, Martin Luther King Jr. was assassinated; Aretha sang "Precious Lord" at his memorial service. At the end of June, she appeared on the cover of *Time* magazine but felt stung by some of the article's unflattering coverage, adding layers to her underlying diffident nature and growing

Opposite: Performing at a Martin Luther King Jr. benefit concert at Madison Square Garden in New York, June 28, 1968.

distrust of the press. Her father faced serious legal troubles back home, and her marriage to Ted White was unraveling. She was arrested later that year for reckless driving and again in 1969 for disorderly conduct.

Artistically, however, she continued to evolve. In tune with popular culture, her look changed from spangly dresses and wigs to natural hair, caftans, and long vests. She'd covered the Rolling Stones and ? and the Mysterians on her second album for Atlantic, but delved more deeply into rock, gravitating toward an audience that was quickly and widely embracing her. On 1970's *This Girl's in Love with You*, she covered the Beatles' "Eleanor Rigby" and

" ' ' ' ' ' ' ' ' ' '

"I just lost my song. That girl took it away from me."

—OTIS REDDING TO PRODUCER JERRY WEXLER AFTER HEARING HER VERSION OF "RESPECT" IN THE STUDIO FOR THE FIRST TIME, 1967

" ' ' ' ' ' ' ' ' ' '

"Let It Be"—which, although he didn't actually write it for her, Paul McCartney ended up thinking should be hers—and brought in slide master Duane Allman to add swampy guitar to her take on the Band's "The Weight." Recorded at the temple of hippiedom, *Aretha Live at Fillmore West* added even more current jams to her oeuvre, including Stephen Stills's "Love the One You're With," Simon and Garfunkel's "Bridge over Troubled Water" (for which she won a Grammy) and Bread's "Make It with You." On *Young, Gifted, and Black*, she covered Elton John's first charting single, "Border Song," and the Beatles' "Long and Winding

Road," but the standout is her own composition "Rock Steady," with its percolating funk, the Memphis Horns, and the Sweethearts of Soul's "What it is" backing vocal refrain.

In 1972, Aretha shifted gears again, taking a nation wearied by war, protests, assassinations, and riots back to church and back to her gospel roots. *Amazing Grace* was recorded at the New Temple Missionary Baptist Church in Watts, with the church choir and full electric band. The album mixed gospel and secular songs, from the traditional "Never Grow Old," which she'd first recorded at fourteen with Joe Von Battle, to an instrumental version of "My Sweet Lord." Religious crossover in rock was omnipresent at the time, with Norman Greenbaum's "Spirit in the Sky," Ocean's "Put Your Hand in the Hand," the Doobie Brothers' "Jesus Is Just Alright," and songs from *Godspell* and *Jesus Christ Superstar* topping the charts in the early 1970s. It was on the small screen as well. While she led the band at New Temple on the second night

· · · · · · · · · · ·

Craig: "Is she a minister?"
Liz: "No, but she ministers!"

—GUIDANCE COUNSELOR LIZ MCINTYRE
EXPLAINS ARETHA ON *ROOM 222*

· · · · · · · · · · ·

of recording, Aretha's episode of *Room 222* aired. One of her few TV appearances, she played Inez Jackson, a spiritual leader who helps a character named Craig deal with his parents' insistence that he become a minister, singing "Guide Me Thy Great Jehovah" with an electric band.

Amazing Grace was a phenomenon for Aretha (more than four decades later, she'd sing the hymn for Pope Francis). It marked the first time she received a credit for her arrangements, and it remains the best-selling album in her catalog. Even audience member Mick Jagger had an epiphany; in Los Angeles to finish sessions for *Exile on Main Street*, he took the gospel influence along with him, and it's audible throughout the Stones' landmark double album. Jagger and Charlie Watts are visible in footage shot by director Sydney Pollack for a documentary on the making of *Amazing Grace*. (The film remains unreleased).

With scattered hits and misses throughout the rest of the decade, Aretha made a big-screen comeback (though she'd never call it that) in 1980 with a cameo in *The Blues Brothers*. She played the proprietress of a greasy spoon who sings "Think" to her cook/husband, played by Matt "Guitar" Murphy, as he's about to take off with the film's titular characters. "She said, 'You know I'm not an actress,'" director John Landis said when he asked her to do the film. "I said, yes you are. You give a performance every time you sing a song. She thought about that and said, 'Yes, that's true.'" Her performance is so vibrant and fun it's a wonder she didn't make more films, though she reprised her role in *Blues Brothers 2000*. This time running an upscale car dealership, she sang "Respect" with two legendary musicians who worked with Otis Redding on the original version: guitarist/producer Steve Cropper and bassist Donald "Duck" Dunn.

By 1982, Aretha was on a new label—Arista—and back in the Top 40 for the first time in six years with *Jump to It* and its supercharged title track. The intersection of pop,

R&B, and disco suited her voice, which soared and scatted, gamboling off the high-gloss production and spiky synthesizers that characterized so much of that decade's music.

The similarly upbeat, contemporary R&B hit "Freeway of Love" from *Who's Zoomin' Who?* put her back in the Top 10 in 1985, as did her duet with the Eurythmics' Annie Lennox and their feminist anthem "Sisters Are Doin' It for Themselves." Her self-titled 1986 album found her playing "Jumpin' Jack Flash" and a keytar with the Rolling Stones, and reaching the top spot on the pop chart via the Grammy-winning "I Knew You Were Waiting (for Me)," her duet with George Michael.

The 1990s consisted of mostly greatest hits compilations and a handful of Grammy-nominated contributions to film soundtracks, until Aretha came roaring back with hip-hop, opera, and a VH1 special to prove that the Queen of Soul retained the crown. Working with Lauryn Hill, Sean Combs, and other young hip-hop and neo-soul artists inspired by her, she released *A Rose Is Still a Rose* in 1998. Hill, then twenty-two years old and several months away from releasing her (only) solo album *The Miseducation of Lauryn Hill*, wrote and produced the title track. The lyrics impart motherly relationship wisdom and self-assuredness to young women, introduced playfully by Aretha's jazz scatting. Borrowing Edie Brickell's "What I Am" refrain—sung by Faith Evans—the song celebrates female collaboration and empowerment, and connects musical genres and generations.

Aretha put her new songs to the test the following month when *VH1 Divas Live* made its debut, with Mariah Carey, Celine Dion, Shania Twain, Gloria Estefan, and a guest appearance by Carole King. She performed the title track and "Here We Go Again" from *A Rose is Still a Rose* (always one to retain her rights, she didn't allow either to be included on the *Divas Live* album or DVD), duetted with Mariah Carey on "Chain of Fools," and basically outsang the most successful and accomplished recording artists of the era. "If you look at the end of it, I was heading towards the backup singers. 'Coz I felt that's where I belonged," Carey said. "When Aretha sings, you don't stand there and try to compete with the Queen of Soul. You revere her."

But her most surprising move was at the fortieth Grammy Awards at Radio City Music Hall in New York earlier that year, when she filled in last-minute for an ailing Luciano Pavarotti, who canceled after the show commenced and was airing live. She was already there to perform for *Blues Brothers 2000*, and the show's producer remembered she had sung "Nessun dorma," the famous tenor aria from Puccini's *Turandot*, at the MusicCares tribute to Pavarotti a few days earlier. Without rehearsal (just a cassette and a few reviews with Pavarotti's conductor), Aretha stepped in front of the fifty-piece orchestra and a thirty-member male choir and left the audience awestruck with her ascending, impromptu aria.

Her final Grammy would come ten years later, a Best Gospel Performance statue for "Never Gonna Break My Faith" with Mary J. Blige. Aretha kept up with contemporary performers and recognized songs that suited her, like Adele's 2010 hit "Rollin' in the Deep." She recorded it for her last studio album, *Aretha Sings the Great Diva Classics* in 2014, and it made her the first woman to land one hundred songs on *Billboard*'s Hot R&B/Hip-Hop chart.

"A lot of people can sing, but the level of artistry that creates an individuality that stands the test of time—there's only a few people on the planet that can do that. And Aretha was one of them." —DAVE PORTER, SONGWRITER

Previous pages: Aretha Franklin promoting her 1987 album *One Lord, One Faith, One Baptism.* **Opposite:** Aretha Franklin portrait, c. 1967. **Above:** Aretha singing "Chain of Fools" on *The Jonathan Winters Show*, 1968.

Above: The Queen of Soul performing on TV in London, 1974.
Opposite: On *The Andy Williams Show*, 1969.

"I stopped shaving my eyebrows and using pencils and went back to a natural look with a much lighter touch. I lost weight and wore my hair in an afro; I began to appreciate myself as a beautiful black woman."

—ARETHA

Opposite: Onstage, c. 1970. **Above:** Aretha Franklin, c. 1970.
Following pages: Singing for the crowd at the National Portrait
Gallery's first fundraising gala (where she was also one of the
honorees), November 15, 2015, in Washington, DC.

Aretha Franklin, 1971.

Above: Rehearsing "Sisters Are Doin' It for Themselves" with Annie Lennox and Dave Stewart of Eurythmics, 1985. **Opposite:** Performing at Radio City Music Hall, 1991. **Following pages:** At Radio City Music Hall celebrating Nelson Mandela's ninety-first birthday, July 18, 2009.

❝Her voice is one of the great natural instruments I've ever heard, and the way she uses it is just so instinctive . . . she knows exactly what she wants.**❞**—KEITH RICHARDS

Above: Posing for the cover of her *Aretha* album, 1980. **Opposite**: Aretha Franklin and Keith Richards, 1987. **Following pages:** On the red carpet in Washington, DC, at the 38th Annual Kennedy Center Honors, the evening of her iconic "fur drop" performance of "(You Make Me Feel Like) A Natural Woman," December 6, 2015.

"I wanted to have a peerless performance. Once I determined that the air [temperature] was all right while I was singing, I said, 'Let's get out of this coat! I'm feeling it. Let's go!'"

—ARETHA ON HER 2015 "FUR DROP" PERFORMANCE AT THE KENNEDY CENTER

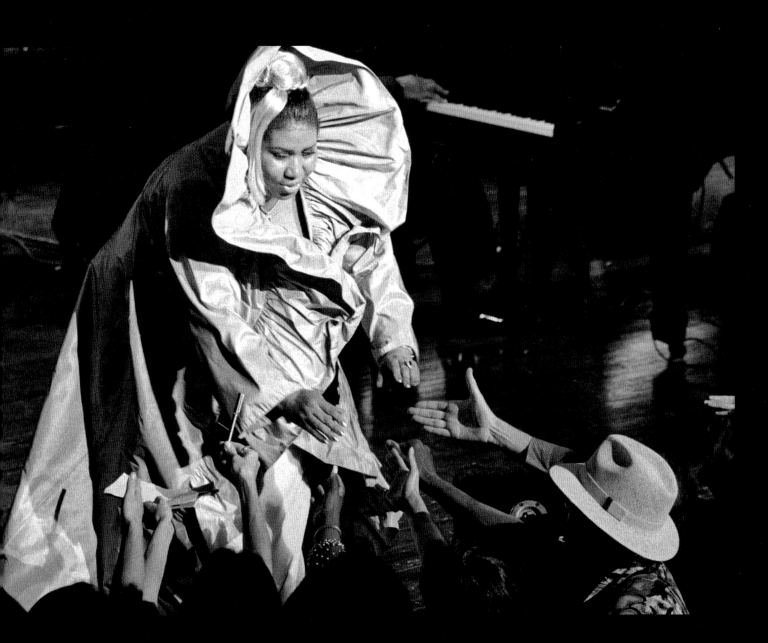

PART THREE

Diva

"ARETHA IS HERE"

By the time Aretha shot *VH1 Divas Live*, she'd already secured her spot as the diva of all divas, the highest point on a crown of jewels, none of whom would be there had she not paved the way. She dominated the stage physically and vocally, even singing over Celine Dion's part on "(You Make Me Feel Like) A Natural Woman"—it was her song, after all. "We had a good time; it was a great night," she later told Oprah.

Just as she'd spent decades seamlessly crossing musical genres, Aretha embodied the word *diva* in every possible sense, from its classical origins (of which she'd proven capable with her stunning aria at the Grammys), to its application in R&B and pop, to its colloquial use to describe demanding talent, to the humorous aspect of being recognized solely by one's given name. "You're in this very rare category . . . all you have to do is say the first name: Aretha is here," talk show host Conan O'Brien joked with her on his show in 2002. "I think only you and I are in this category."

As Aretha defined the term in an interview with *Voice of America*, a diva is "One who is very grand, one who has major credentials, who has sometimes been called difficult, that kind of thing, prima donna, that kind of thing. I suppose I could be that, but only when one is being unfair to me," a mannerly way of expressing that she wouldn't take guff from anyone. If sometimes used in an attempt to demean powerful women, that was not going to work with Aretha—she was ultimately indomitable. "She understood how to wield power without raising her voice," Reverend JoAnn Watson said. "She was paid in advance if she performed. She'd insist there was no air-conditioning if she was to sing. She refused to be extorted or disrespected."

Her diva roots are complex. Part of it stemmed from the care and nurturing of one of the greatest singing voices of all time. The human voice is a fickle instrument, and she needed specific things to get optimal use out of hers: staying out of the aforementioned air-conditioning before performing, quitting cola and chocolate to reduce reflux, "trade secrets" that she never revealed, and other requirements that helped her get into performance mode. It served her well, as her voice lasted a lifetime despite decades of smoking (she officially quit in 1992). Much of it was about respect—Aretha demanded it in song and in life. If she felt disrespected she was vociferous in striking back, whether at a promoter, a journalist, or a record label chairman. There was also the tough exterior she began to cultivate at age nine, when she lost her mother, and growing up fast on the road with her dad's "gospel caravan." That outer shell would only harden as her celebrity grew, further fortifying her diva reputation.

. . . .

"She was the breaker . . . she set the pace for the rest of us."

—GLADYS KNIGHT

. . . .

Although she suffered from insecurities since childhood—her brother Cecil, singer Gladys Knight, Swampers' bassist David Hood, and many others described her as shy and introverted—Aretha gleaned a sense of self-worth from growing up in the gospel community. The warm reception she got from singing in the church emboldened her. On a more temporal level, she was exposed to the "prosperity gospel" of that era. Unlike the bluesmen whose albums shared shelf space with theirs in record stores, gospel singers and reverends had greater control of their own agency. Being spiritual leaders afforded them a certain status without alienating parishioners and neighbors. Though they lived in a mansion, "they were not mansion people,"

as Smokey Robinson said. Aretha often presented this "downhome diva" persona, especially around Detroit, as milliner Luke "Mr." Song observed when she'd visit him for bespoke hats. "She did come with an entourage, in a stretch limo, but other than that, she was down-to-earth," Song said.

Reverend Franklin also paid his teenage daughter $50 a gig to open for him, teaching Aretha a valuable lifelong lesson. Before any concert, she'd take cash up-front, thank you, and keep it in one of the ubiquitous purses that were never far from her, even onstage. As her career took off, so did her sense of her own value. Atlantic had signed her in 1966 for $25,000. When her contract was up six years later, she wanted $5 million to stay. They offered $3 million, then $4 million. Aretha's response? She upped her ask to $6 million, and she got it.

Two of her gospel mentors served as counterbalancing models in creating her diva mystique: Mahalia Jackson and Clara Ward. Jackson had been visiting Reverend Franklin in Detroit for years, keeping an eye on the kids, particularly Aretha; like them, she'd lost her mother at a very young age. Known as the Queen of Gospel and a passionate civil rights activist, Jackson presented a devout image. Large and imposing, often monochromatically dressed in white or black, she refused to sing secular music and divorced her first husband, in part, for his gambling habit. She was a wise investor, buying into real estate and various businesses, and collecting royalties from lending her name to a "glori-fried" chicken and catfish franchise; at the time of her death in 1972, she was estimated to be worth around $4 million.

Opposite: Aretha onstage in one of her bespoke hats.
Following pages: Performing a medley with Tom Jones on his TV show *This Is Tom Jones*, October 1970.

Ward, who Aretha loved like a mother, was C. L. Franklin's girlfriend for many years and sang in their rolling road show. She learned tough business from her mother, Gertrude, a promoter who managed the band and collected the cash, and who outlived Clara by several years. Ward brought the glamour gospel—chiffon gowns in bright hues, furs, and bling. She also brought a little drama, throwing her hat on the ground at the funeral of Aretha's aunt while singing "Peace in the Valley" ("That was when I wanted to become a singer," Aretha later said) and flinging her mink stole at Mahalia Jackson's casket. Like her mentee, Ward was a gifted musical arranger whose group of women singers (including a teenage Marion Williams) traded lead vocals like many male vocal groups at the time. When public interest in gospel music waned, the Ward singers adapted, taking gigs in Las Vegas and Disneyland, playing in New York on Broadway and recording at the famed Village Gate nightclub, and heading to Hollywood, where Ward appeared in films and recorded secular songs.

Aretha found her ground somewhere in the middle. Like Jackson, she was both regal and real, business-minded and altruistic, with the glitz and progressive attitude of Ward. She often insisted on formalities in work situations or speaking in public—she was Ms. Franklin; you were Mr. or Ms. whomever. Her outfits were extravagant and occasionally outlandish, but no matter what she wore, she rocked it, and she defended it. When *New York Post* gossip columnist Liz Smith deigned to write about a dress for which she felt the diva was "too bosomy" in 1993, Aretha quipped back, "When you get to be a noted and respected fashion editor please let us all know." She loved her furs not only for their glamour and for keeping her vocal cords warm, but also occasionally as a prop to drop for dramatic effect while hitting a high note, as she did at the Kennedy Center Honors for Carole King in 2015. And fur wasn't the only thing she'd fling. At BET's 2003 "Annual Walk of Fame," held in her honor, she appeared wrapped in white tulle and glittering crystals. After soul-scatting and vamping through "Respect," followed by "Today I Sing the Blues," she tore off her long wig and tore into the gospel rave "Spirit of the Lord," her real hair slicked back into a small knot.

> "Aretha's always had a fire in her; music's been her ticket to freedom."
> —QUINCY JONES

Some of her more colorful antics were just as much a part of who she was—mercurial, challenging, at times self-indulgent. She walked off *The David Frost Show* mid-interview, excusing herself to smoke a cigarette, even though she was the only guest booked on the ninety-minute show. She threw a $100 bill onto a police desk to pay her $50 bail because she didn't have change, then whirled around and stormed out. She hauled a leaky bag of pig's feet (she loved to peruse neighborhoods and shop for specialty ingredients wherever she traveled) across the lobby of the Fontainebleau hotel in Miami on her way up to their best suite,

Above: Aretha Franklin in concert at Chene Park in Detroit, August 22, 2015.
Following pages: Aretha Franklin performing on a Bob Hope television special in 1975.

where she was staying, ignoring the trotters as they plonked to the floor. There were feuds, fueled by umbrage taken at perceived slights and her highly competitive nature with other female singers. There were the oft-stated plans that never materialized. There were canceled interviews and shade-throwing moments in the interviews that happened.

In the studio, however, the diva made way for the genius. "She was dynamically in tune with what was going on around her. . . . It was never an ego thing at all with her. It was a music thing. She was brilliant in that way I think," Spooner Oldham, who played keyboards on Aretha's early Atlantic recordings, said. She may have shown up on her own time-frame, but she knew exactly what she wanted, was completely prepared, and led the most sophisticated producers and musicians. "Aretha is a perfectionist," Arista president Clive Davis, aka "Mr. Davis," said. "She comes fully rehearsed to the studio. She nails it at that same session. She never does more than three takes. She comes [in after] living with the song before she goes in the studio." Sometimes she'd delay sessions by bringing in barbecue and covered dishes of food she'd cooked for the band, at however many hundreds of dollars an hour it costs for studio time. Of all the diva behavior, that's the best kind—great records are made, and everyone gets to eat.

"I'm not ever going to retire. That wouldn't be good for one just to go somewhere and sit down and do nothing. Please. No, that's not *moi.*" —ARETHA

"I am a natural woman. I think that women have to be strong.
If you don't, some people will run right over you.**"**—ARETHA

Opposite; Onstage at the New Orleans Jazz and Heritage Festival in New Orleans,
April 30, 1994. **Above:** The Queen of Soul in New York during the *VH1 Divas
2001: The One and Only Aretha Franklin* tribute, April 10, 2001.

Above: Arriving at Cipriani Wall Street with partner William Wilkerson (left) and long-time executive producer Clive Davis for Fashion Group International's Night of Stars Gala, October 2013.

Opposite: Franklin shows her stuff for photographers at the 39th Annual Grammy Awards in New York, February 26, 1997.

Above: Aretha Franklin at the 1993 People's Inaugural Celebration. **Opposite:** At the Ritz-Carlton Hotel in New York to celebrate her birthday, March 2015.

In the East Room of the White House singing for President Barack Obama and First Lady Michelle Obama, hosts of Women of Soul: In Performance at the White House, March 6, 2014.

"Nobody embodies more fully the connection between the African American spiritual, the blues, R&B, and rock and roll—the way that hardship and sorrow were transformed into something full of beauty and vitality and hope.

—PRESIDENT BARACK OBAMA

Opposite: Onstage, c. 1986.

Following pages: With a gospel choir shouting out her *Joy to the World* at the Rockefeller Center Christmas tree lighting, December 2009.

"That's a piece of theater, and she's a diva in the best sense . . ."

—CAROLE KING, ON ARETHA FRANKLIN'S PERFORMANCE AT THE 2015 KENNEDY CENTER HONORS

Above: Showing her bling at her birthday celebration, March 2014.
Opposite: At Radio City Music Hall in New York, July 5, 1989.

Opposite: The Mandela Day Celebration Concert at Radio City Music Hall,
July 18, 2009. **Above**: *Divas Live: An Honors Concert for VH1 Save the Music*
at the Beacon Theater in New York with (from left) Mariah Carey, Gloria Estefan,
Carole King (behind Aretha's arm), Aretha Franklin (center front), Shania Twain,
and Celine Dion, April 14, 1998.

“Aretha is a gift from God. When it comes to expressing yourself through song, there is no one who can touch her. She is the reason why women want to sing.”—MARY J. BLIGE

Above: With Mary J. Blige at VH1's *Divas Live: The One and Only Aretha Franklin* at Radio City Music Hall, 2001. **Opposite**: Mariah Carey and Aretha perform during *Divas Live*.

PART FOUR

Honors
& Awards

"IN HER VOICE, WE COULD FEEL OUR HISTORY"

O f all the honors Aretha amassed in her six-decade career, a high point for her was receiving the Presidential Medal of Freedom in 2005. The highest civilian award granted by the United States, it was in recognition of her "lifetime of achievement and helping to shape our nation's artistic and cultural heritage." The ceremony brought Aretha to tears, its emotional intensity heightened by timing. Just a week earlier, she was at the Greater Grace Temple in Detroit, singing at the funeral of civil rights leader Rosa Parks, who'd been awarded the Medal of Freedom in 1996. The word *freedom* itself packs so much power in terms of Aretha's life and career. It was a theme in her classic late 1960s recordings: out of reach in "Chain of Fools," abandoning the artificial constraints of subjective beauty in "(You Make Me Feel Like) A Natural Woman," and as a lyric in "Think," her voice resonating with incremental strength as it climbs the pentatonic scale with each utterance of "freedom."

Since Chicago deejay Pervis Spann crowned her the Queen of Soul in 1967 after "Respect" brought her widespread renown, Aretha has been granted numerous awards for her inimitable, empowering voice and her charitable work, and because she occupies a singular space in music and in popular culture. Gospel was her footing, but it didn't confine her—nothing could, no genre nor ideology. Though "Respect" became a "mantra," as she put it, for social movements, she maintained that it was about all people, and it remains a universal anthem. She was invited to perform at the White House and did so on many occasions, particularly during the Obama presidency, and she periodically endorsed and campaigned for Democratic candidates. Yet the president who placed the Medal of Freedom around her neck was George W. Bush (filmmaker/actor Mel Brooks, for example, passed on the Kennedy Center Honors during Bush's presidency), and she played with his former secretary of state Condoleezza Rice, an accomplished classical pianist, to raise money and arts awareness for inner-city kids in Detroit and Philadelphia.

Previous page: Backstage at the Tenth Annual American Music Awards after winning Favorite Album—Soul/R&B for *Jump to It*, 1983.
Opposite: Aretha Franklin performing at the Lincoln Memorial in celebration of President Bill Clinton's inauguration, January 17, 1993.

Aretha wasn't apolitical; she'd always been involved in political, social, and cultural movements and was frequently ahead of the culture, which ultimately led to more honors. In the 1960s, she helped fund family friend Martin Luther King Jr.'s fight for civil rights. She worked through a difficult performance of the national anthem at the ill-fated Democratic National Convention in 1968; unable to hear the military backing band, who were on the other side of the convention center, she lagged behind the musicians and the crowd, and flubbed the words at one point (people

> "I'll miss clowning with her. Most people don't know the Aretha that could cut up and joke and be a character."
>
> —SAM MOORE, SINGER, SAM & DAVE

freaked out, thinking it was subversive). In the early 1970s, she offered to post bail for Angela Davis, the University of California professor who'd been on the FBI's Most Wanted list and was arrested for kidnapping and murder (Davis was later acquitted on all charges), though the two women never met. She supported Muhammad Ali during his Vietnam protest; a lifelong boxing fan, Aretha was good friends with Ali, who was awarded his Medal of Freedom alongside her in 2005. Four years before the Supreme Court made marriage equality the law of the land, she sang at a high-profile same-sex wedding at New

York's Four Seasons (the officiant was David Boies, who'd successfully argued to overturn California's same-sex marriage ban); she called the couple every year to wish them a happy anniversary. She was outspoken about the gender pay gap and told *Rolling Stone* that women "deserve parity, and maybe even a little more." She called out designers such as Calvin Klein and Valentino for refusing to make plus-size clothing in 1987, long before anyone gave voice to the more than half of American women who are above a size 14. "She was a kind of revolution of her own," singer-songwriter Carole King said. "Her talent, to be sure—a black woman doing her own thing, and leading others around her."

Yet Aretha mostly stayed above the political fray, enjoying the well-deserved status of national treasure. In death, she brought a divided legislative branch together when both Democratic and Republican lawmakers in the House and Senate cosponsored a bill to posthumously award her the Congressional Gold Medal, the nation's "other" highest civilian honor; the last entertainer to receive it was Frank Sinatra in 1997. Who else could unite Senators Kamala Harris (D-California) and Orrin Hatch (R-Utah)? Only Aretha. At fifty-two, she became the youngest Kennedy Center Honors recipient in 1994. Five years later, when fellow Detroiter and close friend Stevie Wonder won his at forty-nine, Aretha collected a National Medal of Arts.

She was an international treasure, too, and might have been even more so were it not for her fear of flying. On November 17, 1980, the Queen of Soul met the Queen of England when Aretha did a Royal Command Performance at the London Palladium. Sammy

Opposite: Winner of the Grammy for Best R&B Female Performance for *Young, Gifted and Black*, 1972.

Davis Jr. introduced her. "We also have royalty in America," he said. "We have the Duke of Ellington, the Count of Basie, and ladies and gentlemen, I bring you the Queen of Soul." She said she'd accepted an invitation to return and was taking a class to overcome her aviophobia, but it never happened. On August 31, 2018, however, just as Aretha's funeral was to commence, Queen Elizabeth II had the Band of the Welsh Guards perform "Respect," much to the surprise and delight of summer tourists gathered outside Buckingham Palace to observe the Changing of the Guard.

Aretha was ever gracious about winning her many music awards, and she never stopped wanting them. The Recording Academy honored her numerous times—eighteen Grammys, the 1991 Legend Award, and the 1994 Lifetime Achievement Award. They also named her MusiCares' 2008 Person of the Year at a star-studded gala, performance, and auction, which raised a record $4.5 million for musicians needing assistance. She won the Grammy for Best Female R&B Vocal Performance eight years in a row and another three times thereafter, giving her the most wins of anyone in that category. And she was thrilled when *Rolling Stone* named her the "Greatest Singer of All Time" in 2008. "That was right out of nowhere. . . . I went 'What?' 'What?' Like a double, triple take. Fabulous, fabulous, thank you, *Rolling Stone*. Unbelievable," she told the magazine in an interview years later. As the first woman inducted into the Rock & Roll Hall of Fame, she made strides for women artists and for her music-rich hometown of Detroit (Motown stars Smokey Robinson and Marvin Gaye were in that 1987 class as well).

She also kept a near-four decade stranglehold on the *Billboard* Top 100 as the female artist with the most appearances (seventy-three, with seventeen in the Top 10) until March 2017, when Nicki Minaj surpassed her.

Honorary degrees, too, seemed to matter a great deal to Aretha, who'd dropped out of high school. She attended many of the commencements, including Berklee College of Music, New York University, the University of Pennsylvania, and the Ivy League schools recognized by one name, like herself—Princeton, Yale, and Harvard. At the latter in 2014, she donned a crimson gown to collect her Doctor of Arts and perform the national anthem for a crowd that included fellow honorees

Above: Doing her best with "The Star-Spangled Banner" at the Democratic National Convention, 1968.
Opposite: With her son Kecalf Cunningham as a section of Madison, between Brush and Witherell, in Detroit is named Aretha Franklin Way in her honor, June 8, 2017.

such as former president George H. W. Bush and former New York City mayor Michael Bloomberg.

It was her home state of Michigan, however, that bestowed upon her the most singular honor, declaring her voice a "natural resource" in 1985. It's hard to imagine anyone else receiving such an accolade—though uniquely hers, it encompassed something even greater. "Aretha helped define the American experience," President Barack Obama said. "In her voice, we could feel our history, all of it and in every shade—our power and our pain, our darkness and our light, our quest for redemption and our hard-won respect. She helped us feel more connected to each other, more hopeful, more human. And sometimes she helped us just forget about everything else and dance."

> "In her voice was shared the joys, sadness, pain and faith of a people. Through the power of her artistry, her voice became universal for all people. You felt that in her music."
>
> —US ATTORNEY ERIC HOLDER

"The secret of her greatness was she took this massive talent and this perfect culture that raised her and decided to be the composer of her own life's song." —BILL CLINTON

Previous pages: Performing at President Bill Clinton's inaugural gala, January 1993. **Above**: Coretta Scott King joins Aretha Franklin at an Arista Records reception for the Queen of Soul at the Ritz-Carlton in Atlanta, October 2, 1993.

Opposite: Aretha Franklin looks on as Jesse Jackson speaks to reporters at the Operation PUSH (People United to Save Humanity) Soul Picnic in New York, March 26, 1972. Behind Jessie Jackson is Betty Shabazz, widow of Malcolm X, and (far right) is Ohio congressman Louis Stokes.

"If it hadn't been for Aretha—and others, but particularly Aretha—the civil rights movement would have been a bird without wings. She lifted us and she inspired us."—REPRESENTATIVE JOHN LEWIS OF GEORGIA

❝When you receive something like the Presidential Medal of Freedom, wow. After God's grace, I'm so grateful for good friends, loyal fans, and the love of the music.❞—ARETHA

Above: Receiving the Presidential Medal of Freedom from George W. Bush at the White House, November 9, 2005.

Opposite: Singing the National Anthem on *NFL Kickoff Live from the National Mall,* in Washington, DC, September 4, 2003.

Previous pages: (Left to right) First Lady Michelle Obama, President Barack Obama, and Vice President Joe Biden watch as Aretha Franklin performs during the dedication of the Martin Luther King Jr. Memorial on the National Mall, October 16, 2011.

Opposite: Aretha Franklin sings at the National Portrait Gallery gala, November 15, 2015. **Above**: At the piano during commencement ceremonies after being awarded an honorary doctorate degree from Harvard University, May 2014.

66We can all learn a little something from
each other, so whatever people can take and
be inspired by . . . is great.**99**—ARETHA

Above: Singer Aretha Franklin performs after being inducted into the Apollo
Legends Hall of Fame, June 2010. **Opposite**: With Lena Horne at the Paramount
Theatre in Madison Square Garden during the Essence Awards, where both were
honored, April 30, 1993. **Following pages:** Singers John Legend and Aretha
Franklin onstage at the Tenth Annual TV Land Awards in New York, April 14, 2012.

Above: Singing "Chain of Fools" at the Kodak Theatre in Los Angeles for the United Negro College Fund telethon, *An Evening of Stars Tribute to Aretha Franklin*, September 9, 2006.

Opposite: In New York with Smokey Robinson and Elton John at a rehearsal for the *Aretha Franklin: Duets* concert to benefit the Gay Men's Health Crisis, April 1993.

Opposite: Celebrating her seventy-second birthday with her son Kecalf Cunningham, March 2014. **Above**: Aretha Franklin's birthday dinner at the Park Lane Hotel in New York, March 2011.

Following pages: Preparing to perform during *The Gospel Tradition: In Performance at the White House*, April 14, 2015.

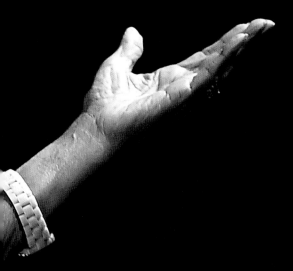

Paying Their
R-E-S-P-E-C-T

THE QUEEN OF SOUL

In the midst of a late-summer heat wave, fans lined up outside Detroit's Charles H. Wright Museum of African American History for one last glimpse of their queen. They had begun arriving more than twenty-four hours before Aretha Franklin was to be on view to the public. Some slept on the sidewalk during the night. Some clutched posters and programs as if they were bringing them to be signed. Bearing ninety-degree temperatures and 70 percent humidity, they were dressed in summer garb, including T-shirts that read "I ♥ Aretha" and "Queen of Soul"—far more casually attired than the star they were there to see.

Early in the morning of August 28, 2018, she arrived in the same white 1940 Cadillac LaSalle hearse that had carried her father as well as Rosa Parks and the Temptations' David Ruffin. The crowd cheered and shouted "We love you!" and "Queen of Soul," and shot photos and video with their cell phones as her solid bronze, gold-plated casket was rolled into the building.

Inside the museum, where Parks was also viewed in 2005, Aretha was surrounded by copious arrangements of roses in pale pink, lavender, and cream, some perched on golden stands. Hairdresser Carlton Northern spent two and a half hours styling her curls into a soft crown. She was dressed in a ruby tea-length chiffon gown with a beaded bodice and matching glossy five-inch Christian Louboutin patent leather heels. Her niece Sabrina Owens said the outfit was "something she would have selected for herself," an indication that Franklin did not plan her denouement (she also died without a will). The crimson

> "She was just consistently a great human being . . . even with whatever turmoil may have been happening in her life. Even through her illness, she did not put that on anybody else."
>
> —STEVIE WONDER

129

color, Owens explained, was for being an honorary sorority sister in Delta Sigma Theta (she was inducted in 1992), whose members filled the Ford Motor Rotunda that night for their Omega Omega Celebration of Life.

For two days, fans streamed slowly past the casket to the sounds of Aretha's gospel recordings. Some blew kisses, some cried, some just stared in disbelief that this woman with a larger-than-life presence had succumbed to humanity's great leveler. Legs crossed at the ankles, she looked tiny in repose. Though she struggled with weight throughout her life, illness had shrunk her to eighty-six pounds near the end. In the months preceding her death, the normally taciturn Aretha had begun to reach out to old friends like Mavis Staples, who said they last spoke in June. "She told me she was going back in the hospital. . . . She told me how she was feeling. When we got off the phone, I started praying because I knew that the time wouldn't be long," Staples said.

Two hours after Aretha passed on August 16, 2018, her eighteen-year-old granddaughter Victorie tweeted a grainy, black-and-white video that looked as if it were recorded on VHS, down to the date stamp of March 17, 2018. Seated by a curtain-covered picture window at her Riverfront Towers condo, Aretha is singing softly, accompanying herself on electric piano and tinkling the keys in a semicircular sparkle of notes to show she

Opposite: Flowers and other items left by fans on Aretha's star on the Hollywood Walk of Fame, August 16, 2018.
Above: The Franklin Street subway stop in Manhattan, August 16, 2018.

hasn't lost her remarkable dexterity. She stops mid-song to blow her granddaughter a big kiss—"Mwah!"—evoking a giggle from Victorie. She looks very thin and a little frail, her hair chopped short, her shoulders rounded as she plays, reading glasses perched at the end of her nose. It was a rare intimate moment with Aretha at home, just six miles from the house on Boston Boulevard where she'd first moved to Detroit as a toddler.

On August 31, Aretha made her final appearance, dressed in a glittering gold dress and sequined gold heels, with golden drapes inside her casket. She reached Greater Grace Temple with a rolling escort of more than one hundred pink Cadillacs, organized by the church's first lady, Crisette Ellis, who drives one herself. A planned program of six and a half hours ran more than eight, featuring eulogies, songs, and stories celebrating her life and legacy. Her family was joined by friends, dignitaries, and stars. Stevie Wonder, Jennifer Hudson, Faith Hill, Bill and Hillary Clinton, Chaka Khan, Cicely Tyson, Yolanda Adams, Ariana Grande, Ronald Isley, Clive Davis, Michigan governor Rick Snyder, Detroit mayor Mike Duggan, and others all walked into the sanctuary through its front doors, no private entrances, no special treatment. Aretha taught the world that all people deserve respect, and everyone was on par that day as they paid theirs to the Queen of Soul.

66My children. And having little get-togethers and making up a whole lot of food. And gold records. And love.99—ARETHA, ON WHAT MAKES HER HAPPY

Above: The Queen of Soul, c. 1969.
Opposite: The Queen of Soul, November 7, 2017.

SELECTED DISCOGRAPHY

STUDIO ALBUMS

1961 *Aretha: With The Ray Bryant Combo* (Columbia)

1962 *The Electrifying Aretha Franklin* (Columbia)

The Tender, the Moving, the Swinging Aretha Franklin (Columbia)

1963 *Laughing on the Outside* (Columbia)

1964 *Unforgettable: A Tribute to Dinah Washington* (Columbia)

Runnin' Out of Fools (Columbia)

1965 *Yeah!!!* (Columbia)

1966 *Soul Sister* (Columbia)

1967 *Take It Like You Give It* (Columbia)

I Never Loved a Man the Way I Love You (Atlantic)

Aretha Arrives (Atlantic)

1968 *Lady Soul* (Atlantic)

Aretha Now (Atlantic)

1969 *Soul '69* (Atlantic)

Soft and Beautiful (Columbia)

1970 *This Girl's in Love with You* (Atlantic)

Spirit in the Dark (Atlantic)

1972 *Young, Gifted and Black* (Atlantic)

1973 *Hey Now Hey (The Other Side of the Sky)* (Atlantic)

1974 *Let Me in Your Life* (Atlantic)

With Everything I Feel in Me (Atlantic)

1975 *You* (Atlantic)

1977 *Sweet Passion* (Atlantic)

1978 *Almighty Fire* (Atlantic)

1979 *La Diva* (Atlantic)

1980 *Aretha* (Arista)

1981 *Love All the Hurt Away* (Arista)

1982 *Jump to It* (Arista)

1983 *Get It Right* (Arista)

1985 *Who's Zoomin' Who?* (Arista)

1986 *Aretha* (Arista)

1989 *Through the Storm* (Arista)

1991 *What You See Is What You Sweat* (Arista)

1998 *A Rose Is Still a Rose* (Arista)

2003 *So Damn Happy* (Arista)

2008 *This Christmas, Aretha* (DMI)

2011 *Aretha: A Woman Falling Out of Love* (Aretha)

2014 *Aretha Franklin Sings the Great Diva Classics* (RCA)

LIVE ALBUMS

1956 *Songs of Faith* (Checker)

1968 *Aretha in Paris* (Atlantic)

1971 *Aretha Live at Fillmore West* (Atlantic)

1972 *Amazing Grace* (Atlantic)

1987 *One Lord, One Faith, One Baptism* (Arista)

1999 *Gospel Greats* (Atlantic)

2005 *Don't Fight the Feeling: Live at Fillmore West (with King Curtis)* (Rhino)

2007 *Oh Me Oh My: Aretha Live in Philly* (Rhino)

ACKNOWLEDGMENTS

Thanks to the unique talents of everyone who put it together, this book is a celebration of Aretha Franklin's incomparable gifts and lasting legacy. Sterling Publishing executive editor Barbara Berger's thoughtful visualization and infinite positivity were inspirational. Night & Day Design's Timothy Shaner created a stunning layout fit for a queen, and photo editor Christopher Measom procured vibrant and compelling images of the Queen herself. Part of the fun of seeing Aretha was about her sartorial choices, whether she was issuing a bold statement on feminism, black power, body image, and Detroit pride, or simply brandishing her bling. Not only do these photos span six decades of style, they also reveal the emotional range of a star known for her reticence—from the rapture she experienced while singing to her contemplative moments.

Also at Sterling Publishing, thank you to Lorie Pagnozzi, art director, interiors, for her insightful direction; Elizabeth Lindy, senior art director, covers and cover designer, for the stunning cover; as well as Kevin Ullrich, creative operations director; Fred Pagan, production manager; and Rodman Neumann, managing editor.

It's fitting that this project was helmed by another sagacious Detroit native—Esther Margolis of Newmarket Publishing Management Corporation; I can't thank her enough for insights from her storied career. Also many thanks to my agent Janet Rosen; my divas Carly Sommerstein, Heather Linson, and Vicki Gilmore; Lita Gottesman and Rhoda Ochs, who are both queens in their own right; the Empire State Soul Club; and, most importantly, Lawrence Ochs, who gives me my propers when he gets home.

NOTES

INTRODUCTION

Page 1: "light a room": Ray Charles; "Lady Soul Singing It Like It Is," *Time*, June 28, 1968. **note for note**: Cecil Franklin; David Ritz, *Respect: The Life of Aretha Franklin* (New York: Little, Brown and Company, 2014). **Elton John proclaimed**: https://tinyurl.com/y8en4f3o. **"It's like electricity"**: Ray Charles; "Lady Soul," *Time*, June 28, 1968. **"down home"**: Smokey Robinson; "Don's Take: Celebrating the Queen of Soul, Aretha Franklin," *CNN Tonight with Don Lemon*, CNN, August 16, 2018, https://tinyurl.com/y92pgjoc. **Who's Zoomin' Who?**: Heather Johnson, "Narada Michael Walden: Grammy-Winning Producer/Artist Honors His Roots," *Mix*, February 1, 2006.

Page 2: "wry, skeptical eye": Dan Aykroyd; https://bit.ly/2DYotTv. **diva medley**: "Aretha Franklin, Impressions Medley," Palais Des Sports, Paris, November 28, 1977, Soul Roulette, published April 27, 2015, https://tinyurl.com/ycnnt9tu. **Her family followed**: Ritz, *Respect*. **father's philandering**: Ibid. **"family wanted for love"**: Mahalia Jackson; "Lady Soul," *Time*, June 28, 1968. **From her 1960s tour:** Errin Haines Whack, "Queen of Soul also leaves a powerful civil rights legacy," *Associated Press*, August 16, 2018. **help fund Martin Luther King Jr.**: Records of the Southern Christian Leadership Conference, 1954–1970, https://

tinyurl.com/y9x4xeu2. **hotel rooms and food**: Adam Graham, "Aretha Franklin pledges help, hotel rooms to Flint, *The Detroit News*, January 28, 2016. **"We didn't buy gas"**: Aretha; Terry Gross, "Aretha Franklin: The *Fresh Air* Interview" (from 1999), NPR, August 16, 2018, https://tinyurl.com/y7vcj3u5.

PART ONE: DETROIT

Page 7: "She was first Detroit's": Dr. E. L. Branch; Chloe Melas, Veronica Rocha, and Brian Ries, "Aretha Franklin's farewell and funeral," CNN, August 31, 2018. https://tinyurl.com/ycu9jvas. **While he entertained**: Interview with Anthony Mason, *CBS Sunday Morning*, May 8, 2011, replayed on *CBS This Morning Saturday*, August 18, 2018. https://tinyurl.com/y7mm3lrl. **he'd used radio:** Nick Salvatore, *Singing in a Strange Land: C. L. Franklin, the Black Church, and the Transformation of America* (New York: Little, Brown and Company, 2005). **Joe Von Battle**: Marsha Music, *A Grown Woman's Tales from Detroit* (blog), "Joe Von Battle–Requiem for a Record Shop Man," November 2008, https://tinyurl.com/y9gwk3ml.

Page 8: "sandbox friend": Aretha; from an unreleased CNN special, clip aired on *Lemon*, CNN, August 16, 2018. **"oil paintings, velvet"**: Smokey Robinson;

NOTES

Salvatore, *Singing in a Strange Land*. **"playing piano and singing"**: Smokey Robinson; *Lemon*, CNN, August 16, 2018. **an adult life**: Ritz, *Respect*.

Page 9: "see who was recording": Aretha; David Malitz, "Post Rock: On the Phone with Aretha Franklin," *Washington Post*, October 22, 2008. **held on to properties**: Louis Aguilar, "10 places in Detroit that helped shape Aretha Franklin," *Detroit News*, August 28, 2018. **Flame Show Bar**: Annalise Frank, "Aretha Franklin: 3 influential appearances in Detroit," *Crain's Detroit Business*, August 16, 2018.

Page 12: "play for the stars": Erma Franklin. *Aretha Franklin—Queen of Soul, Documentary #1*, YouTube, posted by Silvano Mazzella, September 10, 2015, https://www.youtube.com/watch?v=RKfkvbOP1sc. **Detroit Walk to Freedom**: Elizabeth Clemens, "Detroit's Walk to Freedom," Walter P. Reuther Library, Wayne State University, June 16, 2011, https://reuther.wayne.edu/node/7858.

Page 13: food banks: David Malitz, "Post Rock: On the Phone with Aretha Franklin," *Washington Post*, October 22, 2008. **"three or four churches"**: Rev. Robert Smith Jr.; "Detroit leaders, friends remember Aretha Franklin," *Crain's*, August 16, 2018. **Harmony House**: Terri Gruca, "Aretha Franklin once starred in a record chain commercial. Her price? Barbecue and a limo," KVUE-ABC, August 16, 2018,https://tinyurl.com/yddcvsag. **Thanksgiving game kickoff**: Paul Resnikoff, "Aretha Franklin Plays the Longest National Anthem in U.S. History," *Digital Music News*, November 25, 2016.

Page 14: "amongst her people": Rev. Robert Smith Jr.; "Detroit leaders, friends remember Aretha Franklin," *Crain's*, August 16, 2018. **rainbow that appeared suddenly**: https://tinyurl.com/yd4jvdpz. **"only to pray"**: Rev. JoAnn Watson; "Aretha Franklin's farewell and funeral," CNN, August 31, 2018. **"Cancer patients too often"**: Aretha; George "RaStarr" Walker, "Aretha Franklin Celebrates Life and Liberty at John Theurer Cancer Center Benefit at Liberty State Park, NJ," *Impressions Online*, September 30, 2012. **Chene Park**: Edward Pevos, "Aretha Franklin commands respect at hometown Detroit concert," *MLive*, August 23, 2015.

Page 15: "complicated, loving, and giving": Rep. Debbie Dingell; "Detroit leaders, friends remember Aretha Franklin," *Crain's*, August 16, 2018. **possibly being her last concert**: Brian McCollum, "It's mixed emotions for Aretha Franklin ahead of 'possible' final Detroit show," *Detroit Free Press*, June 2, 2017. **moved to tears**: Brian McCollum, "'Aretha Franklin Way' street unveiled for tearful Queen of Soul," *Detroit Free Press*, June 8, 2017. **didn't feel well then either**: Emilia Petrarca, "The Tribeca Film Festival Kick-Off Was Bigger and Louder than Ever Before," *W*, April 20, 2017. **canceling and then recommitting**: Lisa Respers France, "The last time Detroit honored Aretha Franklin," CNN, August 27, 2018.

Page 16: "celebrated and the uncelebrated": Crisette Ellis, Greater Grace Temple First Lady; "Aretha Franklin's farewell and funeral," CNN, August 31, 2018.

Page 21: "acts of kindness and charity": Erma Franklin; Ritz, *Respect*.

Page 23: "Gospel goes with me": Aretha; Gwen Ifill, *PBS NewsHour*, Nov 25, 2015. https://www.youtube.com/watch?v=Vefmg-y4fZ0.

Page 27: "in tune with what was going on": keyboardist Spooner Oldham; Ron Hart, "Spooner Oldham Shares His Memories of Cranking Out Hits with Aretha Franklin in the '60s," *Billboard*, August 28, 2018.

Page 34: "my homegirl": Berry Gordy; Brian McCollum, "Berry Gordy: Aretha Franklin was 'part of my family,'" *Detroit Free Press*, August 17, 2018.

PART TWO: REINVENTION

Page 39: "create a picture": songwriter Dave Porter; Bob Mehr, "Memphis soul veterans mourn Aretha Franklin, recall her musical connections to the city," *Memphis Commercial Appeal*, August 16, 2018. **"a gospel component"**: Ibid.

"a master class": Jon Batiste; *CBS This Morning*, August 17, 2018, https://tinyurl.com/ybsksqnj. **a lifelong crush**: Anthony Mason, *CBS This Morning Saturday*, August 18, 2018, https://tinyurl.com/y7mm3lrl. **his label, RCA**: "*Aretha Franklin—Queen of Soul, Documentary #2*," September 10, 2015, https://tinyurl.com/y9zesw2k. **heard since . . . Billie Holiday**: Ibid.

Page 40: "I'm never singing": Sarah Vaughan after hearing Aretha sing "Skylark." Ritz, *Respect*. **Muscle Shoals, Alabama**: Graeme Thomson, "The Making of Aretha Franklin's 'I Never Loved a Man (The Way I Love You),'" *Uncut*, October 2018.

Page 43: "lost my song": Otis Redding; Lyndsey Havens, "The Best Quotes About Aretha Franklin from Other Singers: Etta James, Mariah Carey, Elton John & More," *Billboard*, August 16, 2018. **wrote for her**: Carole King, *A Natural Woman* (New York: Grand Central Publishing, 2012). **father faced serious legal troubles**: Ritz, *Respect*. **marriage to Ted White**: Ibid. **She was arrested**: Ibid. **"Let It Be"**: Rob Sheffield, "Why Nobody Sang the Beatles Like Aretha," *Rolling Stone*, August 16, 2018.

Page 44: "Is she a minister?" *MeTV* Staff, "Aretha Franklin made one TV acting appearance in her career on *Room 222*," August 13, 2018. **The film remains unreleased**: Steven Zeitchik, "Aretha Franklin's death could finally lead to the release of the world's most sought-after concert film," *Washington Post*, August 17, 2018. **"not an actress"**: Aretha to *Blues Brothers* director John Landis, Mike Fleming Jr., *Deadline Hollywood*, August 16, 2018.

Page 45: "try to compete with the Queen": Mariah Carey; "The Best Quotes," *Billboard*, August 16, 2018. **Nessun dorma**: Andrew Unterberger, "Soy Bomb, ODB, Aretha & the Craziest Grammys Ever: An Oral History of the 1998 Grammys," *Billboard*, January 20, 2018. **kept up with contemporary performers**: Stacey Anderson, "Aretha Franklin Talks Adele Cover, Clive Davis' Influence and 'Real' Singers," *Rolling Stone*, October 2, 2014. **one hundred songs**: Xander Zellner, "Aretha Franklin's Top 20 Biggest Billboard Hot 100 Hits," *Billboard*, August 16, 2018.

Page 46: "the level of artistry": songwriter Dave Porter; Bob Mehr, "Memphis soul veterans mourn Aretha Franklin, recall her musical connections to the city," *Memphis Commercial Appeal*, August 16, 2018.

Page 52: "a beautiful black woman": Aretha; Ritz, *Respect*.

Page 64: "great natural instruments": Keith Richards; *Aretha Franklin—Queen of Soul, Documentary #1*, September 10, 2015.

Page 66: "Let's get out of this coat!": Aretha; Alex Frank, "Aretha Franklin on the 'Natural Woman' Performance that Made President Obama Cry," *Vogue*, January 13, 2016.

PART THREE: DIVA

Page 71: "Aretha is here": Conan O'Brien; *Late Night with Conan O'Brien*, NBC TV (New York), March 27, 2002, https://tinyurl.com/y88ftflr. **"We had a good time"**: Aretha; *The Oprah Winfrey Show*, ABC TV (Chicago), September 30, 1999, https://tinyurl.com/yagjz9ul. **"One who is very grand"**: Aretha; Larry London, *Border Crossings*, Voice of America, October 2008, https://www.voanews.com/a/4532874.html. **"how to wield power"**: Rev. JoAnn Watson; "Aretha Franklin's farewell and funeral," CNN, August 31, 2018. **quitting cola**: Jeff Schwachter, "Aretha Now! Interview with the Queen of Soul," *Atlantic City Weekly*, October 3, 2012. **"trade secrets"**: Frank, *Vogue*, January 13, 2016.

Page 72: decades of smoking: Tanya Basu, "Aretha Franklin's Death Highlights Vicious Path of Pancreatic Cancer," *Daily Beast*, August 16, 2018. **"She was the breaker"**: Gladys Knight; *Lemon*, CNN, August 16, 2018. **shy**: Ibid. **introverted**:

NOTES

David Taylor, "The day Aretha Franklin found her sound—and a bunch of men nearly killed it," *Guardian UK*, August 19, 2018. **prosperity**: Ritz, *Respect*. **a certain status**: "Lady Soul," *Time*, June 28, 1968. **"not mansion people"**: Smokey Robinson; Robin Roberts, *Good Morning America*, August 17, 2018, https://tinyurl.com/y75vq589. **"with an entourage"**: milliner Luke Song; Nancy Kaffer, "Aretha Franklin's Hat" *Detroit Free Press*, August 16, 2018. **$50 a gig**: Gross, "Aretha Franklin: The *Fresh Air* Interview." **cash up-front**: David Remnick, "Soul Survivor: The revival and hidden treasure of Aretha Franklin," *New Yorker*, April 4, 2016. **career took off**: Ritz, *Respect*. **Mahalia Jackson**: "Two Cities Pay Tribute to Mahalia Jackson," *Ebony*, April 1972. **"glori-fried chicken"**: Alice Randall, "Glori-Fried and Glori-fied: Mahalia Jackson's Chicken," *Gravy*, Winter 2015–16.

Page 76: loved like a mother: Ritz, *Respect*. **Clara Ward**: "American Roots Music: Episode Three: The Times They Are A-Changin'," PBS, November 12, 2001, https://www.pbs.org/americanrootsmusic/pbs_arm_saa_clarawardsingers.html. **"wanted to become a singer"**: Aretha; "Lady Soul," *Time*, June 28, 1968. **"too bosomy"**: Liz Smith; Mark Bego, *Aretha Franklin: The Queen of Soul* (New York: Skyhorse Publishing, 2012). **"respected fashion editor"**: Aretha; Ibid. **tore off her long wig**: Veronica Wells, "9 of Aretha Franklin's Most Diva-ish Moments," *Madam Noire*, August 16, 2018. **"a fire in her"**: Quincy Jones; Lois Armstrong and Salley Rayl, "The Blues Brothers Led to a Comeback, but Aretha Franklin Is Still Soul Sister No. 1," *People*, February 23, 1981. **walked off *The David Frost Show***: Bego, *Aretha*. **bail**: Ibid. **bag of pig's feet**: Ibid.

Page 77: "brilliant in that way": "Spooner Oldham," *Billboard*, August 28, 2018. **"a perfectionist"**: Clive Davis, Chief Creative Officer, Sony Music; Melinda Newman, "Clive Davis Reflects on 40-Year Friendship & Creative Partnership with Aretha Franklin," *Billboard*, March 25, 2016.

Page 78: "ever going to retire": Aretha; Ifill, *PBS NewsHour*, November 25, 2015.

Page 81: "natural woman": Aretha; Frank, *Vogue*, January 13, 2016.

Page 89: "hardship and sorrow we": President Barack Obama; Remnick, *New Yorker*, April 4, 2016.

Page 92: "diva in the best sense": Carole King; Ibid.

Page 96: "why women want to sing": Mary J. Blige; "100 Greatest Singers of All Time (Aretha essay)," *Rolling Stone*, November 27, 2008.

PART FOUR: HONORS & AWARDS

Page 101: "feel our history": President Barack Obama, https://twitter.com/BarackObama/status/1030129887623958538. **Pervis Spann crowned her**: Dartunorro Clark, "This is the moment Aretha Franklin became the 'Queen of Soul,'" NBC News, August 16, 2018. **"mantra"**: Aretha; from an unreleased CNN special, clip aired on *Lemon*, CNN, August 16, 2018.

Page 102: fight for civil rights: Rochelle Riley, "Jesse Jackson on Aretha Franklin's quiet but profound civil rights legacy," *Detroit Free Press*, August 15, 2018. **Democratic National Convention in 1968**: Zack Stanton, "When Aretha Franklin Rocked the National Anthem," *Politico*, August 16, 2018. **"clowning with her"**: Sam Moore; "Sam Moore Remembers Aretha Franklin: 'She Was the Greatest,'" *Variety*, August 21, 2018. **bail for Angela Davis**: "Aretha Says She'll Go Angela's Bond If Permitted," *Jet*, December 3, 1970. **supported Muhammad Ali**: Nasir Muhammad, "If you didn't know, Aretha Franklin was a lifelong boxing fan," TheUndefeated.com, August 29, 2018. **same-sex wedding**: Lisa Respers France, "That time Aretha Franklin was the best wedding singer," CNN, August 30, 2018, https://tinyurl.com/ycaybbge. **"women 'deserve parity'"**: Aretha; Patrick Doyle, "Aretha Franklin on Beyoncé, Women's Rights, the Future" (lost excerpts from December 11, 2014 interview), *Rolling Stone*, August 18,

2018. **plus-size clothing**: Channing Hargrove, "Aretha Franklin Was Calling for Diversity in Fashion in the '80s," *Refinery29*, August 16, 2018. **"She was a kind of revolution"**: Carole King; Chris Hayes, *All In*, MSNBC, August 16, 2018, https://tinyurl.com/y7rhzjdm. **brought a divided legislative**: Felicia Sonmez, "Lawmakers introduce bipartisan measure to posthumously award Congressional Gold Medal to Aretha Franklin," *Washington Post*, August 21, 2018.

Page 104: "also have royalty": Sammy Davis Jr.; Roxanne Hughes, "Aretha Franklin's ex-husband reveals shock Queen Mother meeting on *Good Morning Britain*," Express UK, August 17, 2018, https://tinyurl.com/y838c65y. The Band of the Welsh Guards played Aretha Franklin's R.E.S.P.E.C.T on the day of her funeral, on the forecourt of Buckingham Palace, The Royal Family, published September 3, 2018, https://tinyurl.com/y9xqpq23. **2008 Person of the Year**: Chuck Crisafulli, "A Tribute Fit for a Queen," Grammy.com, December 2, 2014. **"Like a double, triple"**: Aretha on being named Greatest Singer of All Time; Doyle, *Rolling Stone*, August 18, 2018. **the most appearances**: "Nicki Minaj Passes Aretha Franklin for Most Billboard Hot 100 Hits of Any Female Artist," *Billboard*, March 20, 2017.

Page 105: "a 'natural resource,'": Susan Whitall, "Aretha Franklin, a performer without peers," *Detroit News*, Aug. 16, 2018. **"universal for all"**: Former US Attorney General Eric Holder; "Aretha Franklin's farewell and funeral," CNN, August 31, 2018. **"define the American experience"**: Barack Obama, http://bit.ly/2y0QNiD.

Page 106: "The secret of her greatness": President Bill Clinton; "Aretha Franklin's farewell and funeral," CNN, August 31, 2018.

Page 109: "a bird without wings": Rep. John Lewis; Tessa Stuart, "Rep. John Lewis: Aretha Franklin 'Moved All of Humanity,'" *Rolling Stone*, August 17, 2018.

Page 110: "good friends, loyal fans": Aretha; Kayleigh Dray, "Aretha Franklin's most powerful and inspiring quotes," *Stylist*, August 2018.

Page 116: "learn a little something": Aretha; *Time* Firsts: The Singer: Aretha Franklin, First woman to be inducted into the Rock and Roll Hall of Fame, https://tinyurl.com/y7xm5fgq.

CODA: PAYING THEIR R-E-S-P-E-C-T

Page 129: "great human being": Stevie Wonder, John Dickerson, Gayle King, Bianna Golodryga, "Soul of a Generation," *CBS This Morning*, August 17, 2018, https://tinyurl.com/yb7y3za9. **one last glimpse**: Kristen Jordan Shamus and Aleanna Siacon, "Fans bid farewell to a Queen: Aretha Franklin," *Detroit Free Press*, August 28, 2018. **Cadillac LaSalle hearse**: Phoebe Wall Howard, "Aretha Franklin's vintage Cadillac hearse also carried her dad and Rosa Parks," *Detroit Free Press*, August 28, 2018. **Carlton Northern**: Mary Chapman, "Aretha Franklin's Hairdresser Styles Her One Last Time," *Daily Beast*, August, 28, 2018. **"selected for herself"**: Sabrina Owens, Aretha's niece; "Sorority hosts packed tribute to Aretha Franklin," *Associated Press*, August 29, 2018, https://tinyurl.com/ydehe9bd.

Page 130: eighty-six pounds: "Aretha Franklin Gravely Ill from Cancer," TMZ, August 13, 2018, https://tinyurl.com/ybkbz3hb. **"back in the hospital"**: Mavis Staples as told to Randy Lewis, "Mavis Staples remembers Aretha Franklin in her own words," *Los Angeles Times*, August 17, 2018. **granddaughter Victorie tweeted**: https://twitter.com/TDirt__/status/1030121065610129408.

Page 132: "little get-togethers": Aretha on what makes her happy; Chris Hodenfield, "Baby, I Know: Reassessing Aretha," *Rolling Stone*, May 23, 1974.

PICTURE CREDITS

Alamy: Pat Benic-POOL/CNP/ZUMA Wire/Alamy Live News: back cover; Christy Bowe/Globe Photos via ZUMA Wire: **110**; Ringo Chiu/ZUMA PRESS: **130**; CSU Archives/Everett Collection: cover, **41**, **103**; Globe Photos/ ZUMAPRESS.COM: **3**, **10**, **17**; Christina Horsten/dpa: **131**; © Nancy Kaszerman/ZUMAPRESS.COM/Alamy Live News: **82**; Pictorial Press Ltd.: **8**, **26**; Roger Tillberg: **30**; © RTKent/MediaPunch: **78**; © RTMarino/MediaPunch: **65**; ZUMA Press, Inc.: **42**

AP Images: © Frank Franklin II: **128**; © Earl Gibson: **120**; © David Guralnick/Detroit News via AP: **105**; © Suzanne Plunkett: **81**; © Charles Sykes/Invision: **122**; © Jim Wells: **109**; © Kathy Willens: **83**

Barack Obama Presidential Library: **86**, **124**

Getty Images: ABC Photo Archives: **74**; Anthony Barboza: **20**, **58**, **59**; Bryan Bedder: **90**; Dave M. Benett: **94**; Walter Bennett/The LIFE Picture Collection: **104**; Bettmann: **99**; Raymond Boyd: **i**; CBS: **49**; Jemal Countess: **116**; Detroit Free Press: **34**; Rick Diamond: **108**; DMI/The LIFE Picture Collection: **117**; Express Newspapers: **15**; Katherine Frey/ The Washington Post: **56**, **114**; Rick Friedman/Corbis Historical: **115**; GAMMA/Gamma-Rapho: **29**; Gems/Redferns: **iii**; Lynn Goldsmith/Corbis/VCG: **60**, **84**; Nicholas Hunt/WireImage: **126**, **133**; Cynthia Johnson/Liaison: **100**; Walter Loss Jr.: **38**; Hiroyuki Ito: **69**; Kevin Mazur Archive 1/WireImage: **96**; Tom Korody/Sygma Premium: **37**; Harry Langdon: **64**; Michael Loccisano: **62**; MANDEL NGAN/AFP: **112**; Catherine McGann: **24**, **121**; Frank Micelotta: **111**; Michael Ochs Archives: **iv–v**, **5**, **6**, **18**, **21**, **27**, **28**, **48**, **54**, **55**, **132**; Monica Morgan/Wireimage: **77**, **123**; NBCUniversal: **51**; Cindy Ord/FilmMagic: **92**; Norman Parkinson/Iconic Images: **22**, **46**, **70**; Al Pereira/Michael Ochs Archives: **88**; Michael Putland: **50**; David Redferns/Redferns: **53**, **80**; Molly Riley/AFP: **66**; Ebet Roberts: **61**, **73**; Fred A. Sabine/NBC/NBCU Photo Bank/Getty Images: **51**; Michael Stewart/WireImage: **85**; Peter Trunley/Corbis/ VCG: **106**; Jack Vartoogian: **95**, **97**; Jerry Wachter/IMAGES: **13**; Andrew H. Walker: **118**; Paul Warner: **35**

Shutterstock: Joe Kennedy/AP: **32**

The Adam Roberts Collection: 9

ABOUT THE AUTHOR

Meredith Ochs is an award-winning radio personality, author, musician, photographer, and deejay. A longtime commentator for NPR's *All Things Considered*, her work has also appeared in *Entertainment Weekly*, *Rolling Stone*, Salon.com, and numerous other publications. Her previous books include *Rock-and-Roll Woman: The 50 Fiercest Female Rockers* and *Bruce Springsteen: An Illustrated Biography*. She lives in Hoboken, New Jersey.